PURE SCIENCE

Thomas Nelson and Sons Ltd
Nelson House Mayfield Road
Walton-on-Thames Surrey
KT12 5PL UK

51 York Place
Edinburgh
EH1 3JD UK

Thomas Nelson (Hong Kong) Ltd
Toppan Building 10/F
22a Westlands Road
Quarry Bay Hong Kong

Thomas Nelson Australia
102 Dodds Street
South Melbourne
Victoria 3205 Australia

Nelson Canada
1120 Birchmount Road
Scarborough Ontario
M1K 5G4 Canada

© Nick Dear 1993
© Andy Kempe for Activities 1993

First published by Thomas Nelson and Sons Ltd 1993

ISBN 0-17-432487-1
NPN 9 8 7 6 5 4 3 2 1

Nick Dear has asserted his moral rights as author of the playscript.

All rights reserved. No paragraph of this publication may be reproduced, copied or transmitted save with written permission or in accordance with the provisions of the Copyright, Design and Patents Act 1988, or under the terms of any licence permitting limited copying issued by the Copyright Licensing Agency, 90 Tottenham Court Road, London W1P 9HE.

All rights whatsoever in this play are strictly reserved and applications for permission to perform it, etc. must be made in advance, before rehearsals begin, to Rosica Colin Limited, 1 Clareville Grove Mews, London SW7 5AH.

Printed in Hong Kong.

Acknowledgement is due to John Aldridge for advising on this series.

ACKNOWLEDGEMENTS
Acknowledgement is due to the following for permission to reproduce photographs:

Mary Evans: p. 51; Ronald Grants: p. 51; Hulton Picture Company: p. 7; Mansell Collection: p. 5, 32, 44; Gerry Murray: p. 51.

Every effort has been made to trace all the copyright holders, but if any have been inadvertently overlooked the publishers will be pleased to make the necessary arrangements at the first opportunity.

CONTENTS

INTRODUCTION iv
FOREWORD vi
CAST LIST ix

THE PLAY: PURE SCIENCE 1

ACTIVITIES 29

FIRST RESPONSES 30
Talking Points **30**
Exploring the Language **33**
Write **35**
Drama **35**

EXPLORING THE CHARACTERS 36
Perkins **36**
Harold and Mary **39**

PERFORMING THE PLAY 41
From Radio to Stage **41**
Designing the Set **43**

ALCHEMY 44
Alchemists and Puffers **44**
The Appliance of Science **48**

DR FAUSTUS 49
A Grisly Tale **49**
Comedy or Tragedy? **52**

INTRODUCTION

DRAMASCRIPTS EXTRA

Dramascripts Extra is a series of plays which can be explored in the classroom, the drama studio or on the stage. Most of the plays in the series were written for performance by professional theatre companies. They are included because their language and structure is accessible to pupils studying English and Drama and because they are concerned with issues relevant to a young audience.

The playscripts are presented in a readable and attractive way without affecting the different styles and demands of the playwrights.

Each play is accompanied by an Activities section which offers teachers and pupils ideas for work which focuses on the play as a written text, the way it might be produced on stage and the themes and issues it explores. The activities cover the Attainment Targets for English at KS 3 and 4 through a range of carefully focused individual and group orientated tasks. Many of the tasks are practical, but while a large room or studio would be an ideal, teachers should find that clearing the desks to one side will give them enough space to tackle most of these exercises.

Andy Kempe, the series editor, taught drama in comprehensive schools for ten years. He is an established author in this field and now lectures in Drama in Education at the University of Reading.

PURE SCIENCE

Haven't we all, at some time, dreamed of having limitless money and knowledge? On the face of it, **Pure Science** is a modern fairy tale about a man who uncovers the secrets of alchemy. Harold has become obsessed with searching for the 'Philosopher's Stone' but Mary isn't quite so sure that the endless life promised by alchemy will necessarily be a good thing. The problem with making stupendous discoveries is that other people might have different ideas about how they should be used. When Mr Perkins arrives and tries to sell the couple 'knowledge' in the form of an incomplete set of encyclopaedias, Harold realises that his 'pure science' can easily be adulterated. You certainly could make a bomb out of such specialist knowledge; and as Harold says, the trouble is, that somebody usually does!

The Activity Section looks at how the subject and language of alchemy has been dealt with previously in literature and how the will to get rich, stay young and simply 'know stuff' still holds people in a spell.

Nick Dear has had a string of successes in the theatre since his play *The Art of Success* won the John Whiting Award in 1986. His adaptations of classic comedies such as *The Last Days of Don Juan*, *A Family Affair*, and *Le Bourgeois Gentilhomme* have been played by the Royal Shakespeare Company and the Royal National Theatre.

A painting of an Alchemist by Joseph Wright. 18th century

FOREWORD

Alchemy has never seemed to me any more obscure and unfathomable than any other branch of science. As far as I can tell all the formulae are gibberish, whether they're for sodium tetrachloride or the Elixir of Life. Maths, physics and chemistry all eluded me completely in the lost weekend of my education. As I came from a family of scientists, this was a matter of some concern at home. My repeated failure to conquer the simplest application of algebra was seen, I think, as some hapless genetic disorder, and was hardly compensated for by my incredible – some would say hysterical – achievements on the acoustic guitar.

So I grew up, a teenager in the Sixties, with an unreasoned but – I fondly thought – a healthy contempt for all forms of science. If science was what your father did, you avoided it like the plague. Science, patently, had caused the Rat Race, the H-bomb, oil slicks and the Vietnam war; it never occurred to me that the fact I hadn't died from cholera at age four had anything to do with it.

Later, though, the bright shining beacon of my ignorance began to fade. I started to wander humbly down previously dark, unexplored pathways in the local library. When no-one was forcing history down my throat, there was nothing I wanted more than to suck it and see what it tasted like. Technology, too, held a fascination for me, though my inability to add up suggested I might never really grasp the finer points.

I read widely of the works of those curious people called Alchemists who, from the time of the ancient Greeks and Chinese, had experimented with a secret and forbidden science. These 'adepts' and their successors invented what we now call chemistry, identifying many previously unknown substances, and changing for all time the way we treat sickness and disease. Their extraordinary goal, though, was the transformation of the scientist himself into some kind of higher being, greater than mere men (they were always men, I'm afraid); they would know they had achieved this when they had created the Philosophers' Stone, an undescribable item with the power of changing base metals into gold, and conferring immortality on its possessor. I learnt that throughout history there had been attempts at this Magnum Opus, this Great Work, and that most of 'modern science' was a spin off. I learnt that many less high-minded types – Grand Princes, in particular – would often try to steal the secret, if it existed, from their court philosophers, and mis-apply its awesome power. It all seemed a very long way from the bunsen burners in the junior physics lab.

One day, years on, I began to write a play about an alchemist who exists in our own day and age, and his struggle to preserve the purity of his 'science with a conscience' from an unscrupulous interloper. At the time I first started writing the play I was much concerned with the nuclear threat. I still am, but the threat has temporarily receded, and small wars with bayonets and little bombs that only kill three or four children dominate the political landscape. But the threat of nuclear extermination will come back. You can't dis-invent something. The play became **Pure Science**, and it was influenced by my discovery that what the ancient Alchemists were talking about – the reduction of matter to its basic elements, and re-arrangement of these to form new matter, new energy – was conceptually the same as our 'modern' particle physics, otherwise known as 'splitting the atom'.

Science may be pure, or applied. We apply it, in my opinion, with insufficient caution. But can you keep it pure? If I was a scientist … but I'm not. I can't add up.

Nick Dear 1993

Splitting the atom. 20th century

CAST LIST

Pure Science was first produced at The Other Place, Stratford-upon-Avon, as part of the Royal Shakespeare Company Youth Festival, 1986. The cast was:

Harold Lamb
David Haig

Mary Lamb
Jane Galloway

Johnny Perkins
Pete Postlethwaite

Directed by
Nick Dear

An earlier version was broadcast on BBC Radio Three. The cast was:

Harold Lamb
Patrick Troughton

Mary Lamb
Elizabeth Spriggs

Johnny Perkins
Derek Fowlds

Directed by
Richard Wortley

For this specially revised version (1993), the extra characters of

The Wordless Book

Harold's Belly, and

An Ancient Chinese Philosopher

have been added by the author. If necessary, though, all these parts can be facets of Harold himself.

THE CHARACTERS

Although both *Harold* and *Mary*, at the beginning of the play, are past retiring age, they should be played by young actors in grey wigs and make-up. Towards the end – for reasons which will become obvious – they shrug off these trappings of old age, and become young again. Their general manner is that of everybody's favourite grandparents.

Perkins is a hard nut in a polyester suit. I wouldn't be surprised if his fingernails were disgusting.

THE SET

The play takes place in the Lambs' house. This looks like any quiet suburban home occupied by a slightly doddering retired couple, with one exception: in the basement there's an alchemist's laboratory. The action takes place in three areas, and it must be possible to cut quickly from one to another. These are (a) the kitchen – equipped many years ago, and arranged neatly around a nice formica table (b) the garden, where Harold grows his weird, exotic plants and (c) the laboratory, a hissing, wheezing wonderland of ovens, flasks and phials, ancient books and peculiar smells. All three locations can be seen at once – in performance, use lighting to jump from one to another, or to slowly fade out of a scene. A great deal of naturalistic detail is not necessary. It's not a naturalistic play.

PURE SCIENCE

SCENE ONE

Just before dawn. **Mary**, *an elderly woman, sits in the kitchen in her dressing gown. Her husband* **Harold** *can be seen in the garden in his work clothes, poring over a dusty ledger in the first streaks of grey light from the east.*

Mary Talk, talk, talk.
Talk blooming talk.
It's all talk.
All night long.
What will become of it?

Harold Page four hundred and nine:

The **Book** *has a voice; it reads itself to Harold.*

The Wordless Book 'The copper man gives and the watery stone receives; the metal gives and the plant receives; the stars give and the flowers receive; the sky gives and the earth receives; the thunderclouds give the fire that darts from them. For all things are interwoven and separate afresh, and all things are mingled and all things combine, all things are mixed and all unmixed, all things are moistened and all things dried and all things flower and blossom in the altar shaped like a bowl.'

Harold Ah, yes, yes, yes, I am getting
the hang of it now.

Mary In the tiny still part of the night
my husband works at his science.
I sit here in the kitchen with my tea and biscuit
to give my legs a rest.
I have bad legs.
They must have gone a million miles for me.
And in my dreams I see
a moving staircase in every home, and golden
moving pavements. Fat chance.
For our unremarkable lives are drawing to an end.
At least, mine is. My man Harold, who I have
known and fed and walked with fifty years,
on these two weary legs,
is certain he will live for ever. Hah! *(laughs)*
Perishing fool.
Talks to himself.
And at dawn you'll find him out collecting dew, yes dew,
down the garden where he grows some

quite unorthodox perennials.
Ooh he is a difficult boy.
He will sit all night in his laboratory
with his thinking cap on his head
and at dawn go out for the dew.
Come in, eat breakfast looking like a washed-up corpse.
I am, he says with a wink, so close to my goal.
Halle-blooming-lujah, says I.
He thinks that I sleep but I don't sleep I listen
out for him
checking he's got everything he needs.
In the matter of keeping body and soul together he isn't
entirely reliable. No.
Blooming good job we are lawfully wed or I wouldn't
stick the solitude! The loneliness! And always
the all-night nattering. Some people
are odd. Who in the world
does he think he's talking to?
Old fool. Who's awake? Who's to hear? Who?

The morning light spreads over the garden. **Harold** *is collecting the dew which has formed on a number of strips of linen laid on the grass. He wrings them out into a bucket.*

Harold Ah! Pure and perfect light!
The sun is not yet up but its golden glow is here
creeping across the earth
like mercury.
The dew must be gathered in the soft grey dawn …
must be filtered through linen
before the sun is risen …
must be left fourteen days in horse dung –

Mary *(watching him from the kitchen, appalled)* Horse dung?

Harold And after fourteen days of deep and holy thinking,
taken out, cleansed of dung,
and distilled to a quarter of its bulk
four times running. The pattern repeated
over and over.
And the books and secret pathways say:

The Wordless Book 'If you are indeed an Artist, you may, by this, turn all Metals into their First Matter.'

Harold *(Looks towards the kitchen.* **Mary** *ducks out of sight)*
Mary old girl I am doing this for you. Though you're

asleep indoors and I'm in the garden
filtering the dew
at the perfect time of the day,
I am with you, beside you,
whispering in your ear.

Mary Twit.

Harold For you suffer me with a laughing heart
and guide me through the darkest tunnels of the night.
One day
this great work will be finished, and then
we shall fear no more the cold and the damp of
the box in the earth
or the heat of the white hot furnace.
The world, beyond the trellis at the bottom of the lawn,
is a sour place, full of
bitter people.
O there is plenty to dread.
Ancient as we are.
But if we can hold on … if we can
sit it out, Mary, you and me, with cups
of tea and sandwiches and shelter from the rain,
then there are days of luxury to come –
I promise you!
It is in my power!

***Harold** goes off with his bucket of dew.*

SCENE TWO

*A little later. **Mary** is still in the kitchen. She pours herself another cup of tea.*

Mary Once upon a time I would always listen in to the wireless after my husband had gone off to his work. But Harold's home for ever now and we have breakfast together of a morning, me just up and him on his way to his slumbers. And he couldn't stomach it you see. The wireless. Boot Lickers, Yes Men and Liars were the words that sprang to his lips, and that was before 'Yesterday in Parliament' had even started. For politics, he said, and the news of the world, gave him a squiffy bowel. Which to me was something of a comfort, as for a spell it'd seemed my cooking was under suspicion. But no. 'Twas the men of power, the women of wealth. And it sets you thinking. And do you know, Harold hadn't been retired a week when my tummy started playing up too! So we have silence now, and, well what can you say, but I have grown to like it.

Long pause.

Yes, I like it.
If you are honest
it makes a lot more sense
than the endless dribble of the wireless.

The doorbell chimes.

Coming! – Drat. Who can that be,
and me not even dressed?

*She shuffles to the door in her slippers. Outside is **Perkins**, smiling and holding a very heavy leather-bound encyclopaedia.*

Mmm?

Perkins Good morning, good morning, a fine, clear, almost perfect morning, madam, don't you think? You must agree and your tulips look a treat. Did you know there are three hundred and forty thousand different word-types in the English language?

Mary Cor.

Perkins An astonishing fact, a gleaming jewel in the crown of knowledge, wouldn't you admit? Eh? Course you would. Even Shakespeare himself in all his plays and novels could only manage to use twenty-nine thousand and sixty-six of 'em. How we lesser mortals communicate at all is the big question of the day.

Mary Oh um.

Perkins Makes you wonder does it not? What's a palindrome?

Mary Eh?

Perkins Palindrome, palindrome, come come, chop chop, Napoleon's Lament. No? 'Able was I ere I saw Elba.' Palindrome. Reads the same word-wise forwards or backwards. Try it.

Mary Ooer.

Perkins See? Right. Shortest English sentence containing all twenty-six letters of the alphabet.

Mary Er …

Perkins 'Jackdaws love my big sphinx of quartz.'

Mary That's thirty-one.

Perkins Eh?

Mary Thirty-one letters in that.

Perkins Bloody hell. The bloody book's bloody wrong.

Mary What book?

Perkins Here we are look. *(He shows her the encyclopaedia.)*

Mary Ah-hah. So that's your little game.

Perkins Read this. Your life will never be the same.

Mary My life is as I want it, thanks.

Perkins Your legs don't look too clever.

Mary Good morning. *(She tries to close the door)* Oh! Please remove your foot!

Perkins I can't, it's stuck to my …

Mary Or shall I call a bobby?

Perkins No don't. My card … *(he gives her his card)* John Perkins is the name.

Mary *(Trying to push him out of the door)* They've warned us off men like you.

Perkins No they haven't.

Mary Yes. In the Post Office.

Perkins See this encyclopaedia …

Mary On the telly.

Perkins It's very very heavy and very good value …

Mary Collapse of civilisation. Door to door community bobbies we have got, with rolled-up sleeves and christian names. Seen their picture in the butcher's. They'll be along in a minute. Regular as you like. They're on the lookout for imposters.

Perkins I am just what I appear to be, madam, here, feel for yourself, look at the photographs, point at the words, there's weightiness for you madam, there's pounds and pounds of …

Mary *(shouts and struggles)* Help!

Perkins … knowledge. *(The book falls)* Yow! You've dropped it!

Mary Sorry.

Perkins On me toes!

Mary Oh, you better come in then, I suppose.

Perkins grins, retrieves his encyclopaedia and hops inside on one leg.
Mary follows. Blackout.

SCENE THREE

At the same time, Harold is at work in his laboratory. His apparatus is chugging away quietly behind him. He pores over the Wordless Book.

Harold Now, where were we?

The Wordless Book 'The investigation of perfection.'

Harold Ah.

The Wordless Book 'This science treats of the imperfect bodies of materials, and teacheth how to perfect them. We therefore in the first place consider …'

Harold *(yawns)* Yes, yes, I'll consider. But must I run the experiment yet again? From the beginning? I am too well accustomed to defeat and now suddenly I am old. And how does Mary cope with these disappointments? Every year, since our marriage, another setback, another great darkness, and every penny squandered upon it. We skimp and save, but Mary stays constant, Mary stands firm, I don't know why. I'm surprised she hasn't left me. Dear Mary. *(yawns again)* Oh, I can't read any more, my glasses have steamed up. Or is it my eyes, misting? It's been a long night, my head is fuzzy and my belly calls out for its breakfast:

Harold's Belly also has a voice.

Harold's Belly *(a rumbling call from somewhere cavernous below)* I'll have bacon egg and tomato, toast, marmalade, and a pot of your wife's excellent tea.

Harold I devote my life to the pursuit of absolute knowledge and this imperfect body thinks only of its grub. The world is a mercenary place.

Harold's Belly *(sardonic)* As above, so below.

Harold As above, so below. Let us finish for tonight, and go and wash and eat. Come, stomach, for a last scrutiny of the apparatus.

He tinkers with his experiment.

I have witnessed now every stage of the work

bar one.
I have performed all of the preparations:
calcination, sublimation, distillation, putrefaction,
and yet still I stand empty-handed and
humble, a bumbling old man in a cellar,
with his foot in the door of forever.
Listen to the tools of immortality.
Heating and cooling, and heating again.
Here is the furnace, here is the egg,
sealed and secret glass, the philosophers' phial,
from which our hope it is to hatch the Stone.
Oh, it's all fairy language, but it does no harm.
It's no more mumbo jumbo
than H_2O or atomic numbers.
For this our chemistry is but a map,
stations passed
on another journey.
My travels.
The scientist's reflected in his science, and
each stage of this progress is charted by a colour.
Colour follows colour in ancient order.
This is the way:

He takes us on a tour of the experiment, pointing out the coloured liquids which represent the various stages of the experiment.

First the black putrescence.
The Matter is reduced to what it was
before it was the Matter.
Forty days of darkness.
Then the Peacock's Tail, so beautiful:
a multitude of rainbows in a bottle, or
all the oils of the earth
co-mingled in a sunlit puddle.
Twenty days of this.
Days of hope.
Next comes the white:
Luna, the Moon, increasingly bright, the whitest
white ever, and then with a little more fire, in
the heat of the Dog Days, the Yellow stage:
a mad excitement damped with prayer.
Weeks turn into months, and quick as you like
a lifetime is spent.
Good heavens, look at this!

He notices something which astounds him: the final flask has turned a deep, fiery red.

The first hint of the last colour –
the beginning of the end –
The Red!
Success!

Blackout.

SCENE FOUR

Simultaneously, **Mary** *and* **Perkins** *are in the kitchen.* **Perkins** *is sitting with his foot up on a chair, as* **Mary** *bustles around him.*

Mary How's the foot, Mr Perkins?

Perkins You can call me Johnny.

Mary Does it hurt? Some tea perhaps?

Perkins If you had it …

Mary Yes?

Perkins I might well drink a coffee.

Mary Right.

Perkins It's more in keeping, you'll agree, with my executive lifestyle. But I doubt coffee alone will ease the pain.

Mary How about some cornflakes?

Perkins A rasher of bacon, I was thinking, ought to do the trick.

Mary Bacon. Egg? Egg and bacon. Hate to see a body sick.

Perkins Pardon my socks if I take my shoe off.

Mary Is it swollen?

Perkins Nah. Well, not so's you'd notice from over there – but it's turning blue, inside my sock, and throbbing, that I guarantee. Cross my heart and hope to die, them volumes weigh a ton. Now if one of them on its own can expand the capacity of my pedal extremity, thus, think what the whole set could do for your brain, yes, ingested slowly bit by bit, and paid for on the never-never if you like, sign here.

Mary Well I don't know …

Perkins 'S a bargain!

Mary Well I'm just a housewife.

Perkins What about your grandchildren? Do it for them! Don't you care about your grandchildren? Eh!

Mary Really reading's not my thing. And my husband is the one with the signature. My husband thinks an awful lot, you'll have to talk to him.

Perkins He up?

Mary He's round about.

Perkins Magic.

He settles down to wait.

SCENE FIVE

In the lab, the equipment's going berserk. So's **Harold**. *He ecstatically raises a flask of the red liquid.*

Harold I've never seen it before!
Red for tincture, red for stone!
Some arcane power held in my hands,
touching and trembling, body, belly, brain and heart,
all one in the bright light of the lion's blood –
the fiery vermilion!
the red poppy of the rock!

Various glass retorts explode around the lab. Flashes of light, sparks, smoke. **Harold** *cries out as glass cascades around him. Then there's an awed silence, and the low moan of a distant wind.*

The egg has cracked.
The stone is born.
That smell ... the secret perfume of wisdom ... like
fresh earth on a June morning, and flowers coming into
bloom, and dew, and wind over heather ...

We will drink.
Mary, we will drink the mercury of the philosophers.
Or you might say
the Elixir of Life.

He drinks a long draught of the red liquid. Fade out.

SCENE SIX

In the kitchen, **Mary** *puts a plate of food in front of* **Perkins**, *who wolfs it down.*

Perkins Mmm. Looks all right, that.

Mary You start work very early, Mr Perkins.

Perkins I thought I saw your hubby in the garden, that's the reason, carrying a bucket.

Mary You're a chap who seems determined.

Perkins Yes I am.

Mary You seem to know the things you want from life.

Perkins Correct.

Mary My Harold's like that too; but what it is he's after I have never sort of fathomed. Whereas you in your ice-blue suit …

Perkins I am a man with a mission.
I am the bringer of leather-bound knowledge
to the warring and ignorant mass.
I like to think I am a useful bloke.
'Cause I perform a function. Men like me
are sorely needed in our sick society.
For I have the wisdom of the ancients,
going at a knock-down price.

Mary How public-spirited! What's in it for you?

Perkins What's in it for me? What are you suggesting madam?

Mary Well, you don't do it for love, never in a million years.

Perkins Who says?

Mary Well how do you make a living, dear?

Perkins It's a doddle. There's always someone wants to suss
the secrets of the universe, and after half an hour
with me, their little heads are fairly burning,
for I have bunged 'em full of academic learning,
and they're on their knees for more.
I take my crusade bloody seriously for
I am a sort of guru to the system's rejects.
Them without references, them without prospects,
they can look to me for self-advancement –
here's nineteen volumes geared to life-enhancement!

Here's facts, figures, vital statistics,
primeval slime to nuclear fission!
Pay cash, cheque book, credit card or banker's
order. I'm all right. I'm on commission.
I've creamed off my percent
of every sentence ever written,
become a door-to-door computer bank,
the brain of bleeding Britain!
See what I do
is I make you
look dim if not remedial –
and then I explain how for relatively few weekly payments
you could develop assets on a par with mine, that is to say,
encyclopaedial.
Like I said, it's a cinch.
Did you know a dying octopus often eats its own arms?

Mary Ooer, Mr Perkins! You're all in a froth.

The exhibition of his own genius has left Perkins drooling and sweating. But he mistakes her meaning.

Perkins *(laughs)* You're half-undressed yourself Mrs.

Mary I beg your pardon! They're my pyjamas!

Perkins Well, you wouldn't be the first to try and get yourself a discount.

Mary Young man I am an O.A.P.!
What you suggest has quite disgusted me.
I cooked your blooming breakfast, now eat it and be gone.
I'm off upstairs to put some clothing on!

*Exit **Mary**.*

Perkins *(eats, sourly)* Wey-hey, I like a bit of meat.
Seed of chicken, juice of cow,
I like to think me innards is replete.
Profit is profit and I don't care how
I bloody got it. As for me feet
there's sod-all wrong with 'em. I had to cheat
to get where I am now, it's me modus operandi.
I dropped the bastard book meself.
In the search for untold wealth
I have found my lack of scruple
to have come in very handy.

Harold enters the kitchen. Several of his teeth have fallen out, as have great tufts of his hair. He is blackened with smoke.

Harold *(calls)* Mary! Wifey!

Perkins Good morning, sir, good morning.

Harold There's a fellow here eating my breakfast!

Perkins Johnny Perkins is the name, and I'm in business.

Harold Business? Phew! I thought my gut had taken on another human form.

Perkins See your good wife …

Harold Oh you've introduced yourselves?

Perkins Yeah, yeah.

Harold So you're not a burglar either? Well fine. How do you do.

Perkins John Perkins or just Perky for short. *(They shake hands)*

Harold Ah yes. Harold Lamb. I'm retired you know. Easy target for a diddler or a confidence man.

Perkins Not at all, not at all.

Harold Excuse me, I've been all night at my studies. I have to wash my hands before I eat.

Harold washes his hands in a bowl of water at the sink.

Perkins You know, Mr Lamb, it's a miracle of nature, that.

Harold What is?

Perkins Water. Water is a thing I have a thing about. I mean it is everywhere, is it not? Even a man like me is partially composed of it. There is an eternity of the stuff. How much of the world's surface, would you say, offhand, was wet?

Harold Offhand, seventy-one percent.

Perkins I knew you wouldn't have a clue, very few punters ever do, the answer is – oi. Did you say seventy-one percent you brainy old sausage?

Harold *(eating cornflakes)* Yes I did.

Perkins Well how the fiddley diddley do you know that?

Harold I am a sage. Pass the sugar, there's a good fellow.

Perkins *(cross)* Pleasure.

Harold Ta. And if you're full I'll have that rasher.

Perkins *(aside)* Got a right one here John boy.

Harold Water is one of the four elements.

Perkins Too true my son.

Harold That's how I know the answer to your question. I take a professional interest. For the four elements give form to the prime matter – the basis of our entire material world. Now this idea, you see, Mr Perkins, comes from the work of the philosopher Aristotle.

Perkins Oh, him, yeah.

Harold Aristotle is known to you?

Perkins Great thinker, great thinker. 384 to 322 BC. – Now what was it he thought *about*?

Harold Earth, air, fire, water.

Perkins Basis of everything. Right.

Harold Dry, moist, cold and hot.

Perkins *What* do you do in the depth of the night?

Harold I read a bit, and think a lot.

Perkins And fiddle with your elemental forces, hey?

Harold I need more tea. Mary!

Mary *(off)* Coming!

Harold She's a good wife, you know.

Perkins She'd have to be.

Harold I'm not very hot on cooking.

Perkins About these studies down below …

Harold Did I say that exactly?

Perkins No.

Harold Where is my wife? I've a surprise for her.

Perkins Here, while you're waiting, cast your eye on this encyclopaedia.

Harold What would *I* want with a thing like that?

Perkins Oh, people get to treasure it …

Mary enters, now dressed.

Mary Morning, Harold, sorry I'm – WAAAAGH! Oh what have you done you blooming nit?

Harold What's up?

Perkins Yeah what's your problem?

Mary Oh Harold, Harold …

Harold But Mary dear, the news is good!

Mary What! With half your teeth gone missing, and your hair coming out in clumps?

Perkins Didn't he always look a bit mothy?

Mary I wouldn't spend fifty years with a man who looked like that! Credit me with something in the IQ department, please!

Harold *(pulling out tufts of his hair)* Crumbs, I hadn't noticed.

Mary We'll be oysterised. We will. Nobody will want to know us.

Perkins *(aside)* Domestic crisis. Just my luck.

Harold Mary, please don't cry. This is the finest thing that's ever happened.

Mary *(sobs)* Is it?

Harold I have attained my goal. I am transformed.

Mary Listen to him. Transformed.

Harold Yes! It's fantastic!

Perkins What is fantastic about senile decay, my rapidly balding friend?

Harold Can't tell you. Shouldn't be talking at all. Should be calm. Pride! That's the culprit. No, you wouldn't understand, young man – please go.

Perkins What, me? Not understand? My antennae is atwitch. You have nearly let the pussy out the bag, haven't you? Now if it's a question of money …

Harold No! Please leave, if Mammon is your god.

Mary You stop still Mr Perkins. I want someone sane around here if my husband's going off the deep end. Harold I've just about had enough. I'm not spending the last of my days mashing your food and combing your toupee. I deserve more than that, Harold – don't I?

Harold *(meek)* Yes.

Mary Ooh you make me livid! I suppose you're going to tell us you've found that perishing stone you've looked for all these years?

Perkins What stone is this?

Mary It's all mixed up with the collecting of the dew, Mr Perkins, that he does of a gloomy dawn.

Harold I'm off dew.

Mary Off dew are you?

Perkins Led you up the garden path, did it?

Harold Yes. But today the search is at an end.

Mary That means he must of stumbled across this bit of rock this morning. He tends to talk in riddles.

Harold Now watch your flapping tongue, my dear …

Perkins Flap on. I've lost the thread.

Mary The stone. The blooming stone, I said. The Philosophers' Stone …

Harold No more!

Mary … that changes lead to yellow gold. Hah! *(scathing)* You've found it, have you, Harold?

Perkins The Philosophers' Stone? You're either bonkers …

Harold I am not mad!

Perkins … or you're a bleeding alchemist my son.

Harold I am a man of science! Alchemy is a science! *(pause)* Vanity of vanities, all is vanity …

***Harold** hurries out. **Perkins** and **Mary** look at each other.*

Perkins Well, you could knock me down with a feather, Mrs. Your husband is a man after my own heart, in his search for the glittering goldbricks. Now as luck would have it I've perused an entry or two upon this very subject. If a true Artist he be, we shall soon discover it. You better make another pot of tea. I fancy I can see a bit of an opening here … **Fade out.**

SCENE SEVEN

Perkins is poking around in the laboratory. The apparatus is quieter than previously. It pulses gently like a sleeping animal.

Perkins Somewhere down here is the basement of hell.
Let us have a butchers.
– Lord what's that smell?
What's that equipment for? That wordless book?
Old Harold's got it made down here. This cosy
little nook smells more like a florist's than
the region of the damned.
I'm afraid the old codgers did become kind of stroppy.
But they clammed up pretty quick when I mentioned
my mate Bobby with his lorry-load of ready-mix,
and his delinquent trick of spreading it like
jam on peoples' lawns.
He's a lad, is Robert.
Even so, this concrete threat
did not completely fright my new-found friends upstairs.
So I had to tip creosote over the rockery
as a foretaste of the grief that could be theirs.
A liberty, yes. But you can't make a mockery
of free market forces.
It is not right. I mean we might be sitting on
a goldmine, yet
the old miser wants it all for hisself.
I ask you.
In legal business you would call it a monopoly,
or even a bourgeois hegemony if you was really narked,
and this is one of the causes
of decent blokes like me, an' Bobby, being left out
in the gutter.
For, to tell as near the naked truth
as old Perky is likely to be heard to utter,
I'm skint.
I'm up to me nostrils in debt.
The heavy books caper is right down the pan.
Specially seeing I'm eighteen volumes short of a set.
Oh, I take a down-payment here and there, where I can.
And I know how to deal with a difficult client.
A dink! an' a wallop! will leave 'em compliant
an' clutching me fountain pen, ready to sign,
in a quivering hand on the old dotted line …
whilst I have a rummage through the sideboard.

Pensioners are my primary targets.
Everyone else has got home computers, yeah,
and video cassettes, and has no time
for books and suchlike literary stuff.
I firmly believe the society that invented
those bleeding electronic gadgets
owes me my compensation.
But anyone under seventy tends to cut up rough
when I suggest participation
in my private pension scheme.
So I've become a mean old wolf. I hunt and howl.
I have abandoned honest toil.
It doesn't bloody pay.
'Cause who wants general knowledge, like, today?

Right lot of peculiar junk in here.
Bottles, bellows, crucibles, tubes and flasks,
and this *(the elixir)*, the deepest red I've ever eyeballed.
Fire, water, broken glass and iffy odours …
All needed for the magnum opus, so I'm told.
But where the blinky blimey are the bars
of bleeding gold?

SCENE EIGHT

Harold and Mary are digging in the garden. Mary is on her knees with a trowel. Harold leans on his shovel to rest.

Harold In ancient China, the Adepts had a code:

A gong sounds. An Ancient Chinese Philosopher appears, accompanied by the sound of cicadas and soft wind in willow trees.

Ancient Chinese Philosopher 'Never allow soldiers, princes or politicians to witness the Great Work. Our science is a secret, for each investigator to discover alone. Do not even let an insect in the room where you are working!'

The gong sounds again, and the Ancient Chinese Philosopher disappears, perhaps in a puff of smoke, who knows?

Harold And now we have this creature in our house, in our garden. Between us, you in your anger and I in my pride, we have opened the great window to a beast without a soul.

Mary He can't know the cost of creosote, either. He used a whole drum. Ooh, the state of this topsoil! I can't stand a man with no respect for plants.

Harold But how do we send him away?

Mary I'm ever so sorry, Harold. Blurting it out. I thought it was all fairy tales. Thought it went out with knights in blooming armour. Thought you, dear, were just making smells with your chemistry set.

Harold Fifty years? Making smells?

Mary Well what *were* you doing down there to make your teeth and your hair fall out?

Harold That's a sign. A prelude to eternity.

Mary We're going to live for ever, are we?

Harold Yes. I have the red elixir.

Mary … And you'll make some gold, dear, will you, now?

Harold Shouldn't think so, no. Can't really see the point.

Mary *(getting cross)* The point? Harold, how long do you think they'll go on paying us a pension?

Harold Do they pay us a pension? I didn't know.

Mary What do you think we live on?

Harold Mary, don't pester me with these details now. I've far too much on my mind. Don't you see I've come awake? I've come alive! Grown my wings … a bursting chrysalis … and you'll change, too! I will show you, and you will see!

Mary I see already. The sickening curve of the daily round. The monotony, Harold. The grinding. See it through a kind of fog. Painkillers, sleeping pills, too many cups of tea. When you get old they get you hooked on blooming everything. My legs ache, my hands are chapped, the darns in my stockings itch. It's been fifty years. I dream … once, just once in my life I would love to wear gold … next to the skin … and drink, oh, I don't know – champagne! And dance again, and sparkle. *(pause)* But the government … this government doesn't care about my dreams, and the pills just make me worse, and my shopping trolley's got all rusty, and on top of everything it's ruddy difficult living with you!

Perkins approaches fast.

Perkins Are we digging for treasure, are we? Are we digging for the buried gold in the secret place? Or what are we about?

Harold Getting rid of the creosote.

Perkins You what? Speak up.

Harold That you poured on the alpine plants.

Perkins Ah, you shouldn't take life so serious. A plant is just a plant, though I'll concede your alpine lichen is an interesting item, being as it lives on naught but mountain air. But I am not at all like that, my geriatric friends. Mere oxygen alone will not sustain a Perkins. I am a man of certain needs, the chiefest of which is money. Now come on pull your fingers out!

He pushes Harold to the ground.

Harold Mr Perkins, there isn't any gold. To an alchemist, the stuff is terribly insignificant.

Perkins Don't come it existential, chum. Think concrete, right?

Harold I've never made any gold! The ancient art is a science which exalts man, not matter! Our real purpose is not the transmutation of metals, but the transformation of the alchemist himself. To a higher state of consciousness. To deification.

Perkins Look, I happen to know that a hundred thousand manuscripts exist on this one subject! I hardly think they'd of got written if that was all it bloody was. *(sneers)* Deification. Who wants to be a bloody god? There must be some material results or why would you bother?

Harold I don't deny that. It can be done. But the material results are only a symbol of something which is spiritual, if you have any tiny notion of what that means.

Perkins threatens him with the shovel.

Mary Don't hit him, Mr Perkins! John!

Perkins Look, Harry, I have read it up! In me book! Under 'A'! And I know there's something going off here that I have not been in on!

Mary Me neither.

Perkins *(to Mary)* It must be feasible. The transmutation. I know it's feasible.

Harold … It is dangerous.

Perkins Why?

Harold When matter is reduced to its primary state, great forces are unleashed.

Perkins You're talking about your sub-atomic oojahs.

Harold I am. With experiments of this nature … the release of energy is potentially huge … terrifying …

Perkins Nuclear.

Harold Yes.

Mary Ooer.

Perkins I reckon nuclear power's the best thing to happen to a dreary little planet since the invention of the wheel. Somebody, blimey, somebody must be making a bomb!

Harold Somebody usually does.

Perkins Don't get cynical! I cannot stand a cynic.

Harold Alchemists have a right to be cynical. Alchemy has for centuries known secrets that you think to be new, and that would better still be hidden. Oh, we gave warnings, we said, look, this stuff is jolly delicate, and what happens? Hiroshima. Who would give them the secret? The businessmen, the soldiers. The mischief-makers. The women of war. Who would give them the elixir of life?

Perkins The elixir of life? Do you mean there are blokes wandering the globe who've been at the base-metal-into-gold caper for … hundreds of years?

Harold Thousands.

Perkins Harold, Harold, you can't keep a thing like this to yourself, it's immoral! With all that gold, everyone in the world could give up work! You've got to tell me how it's done! *(He shakes Harold by the throat)*

Harold You will never possess our knowledge! Not in the cold stone of your heart!

Perkins You intransigent bastard!

Harold We learn to keep our secrets. The noisome world keeps turning. We live on in peace and stillness with our female guides.

Mary That's all I get to do, is it? Be the blooming guide? Oh thank you very much. And feed your rumbling belly, eh? And you get all the credit? It's not much to offer me, Harold, in the fag-end of my life.

Harold But we can live for ever!

Mary Who wants to live for ever? It's dull!

Harold Dull?

Mary And flippin' hard work!

Perkins Too right. It's unpaid labour, madam.

Harold Fifty years …

Mary Yes fifty years!

Perkins And treated like a drudge.

Mary Mr Perkins, I'm with you.

Perkins ⎫
                      ⎬ *(together)* What?
Harold ⎭

Mary You've widened my horizons. My fancy's tickled by your world of leisure, if it means that I can take the burden off my legs. The thought of languishing in luxury does wonders for the circulation. Come down underground to the lab. His secret words and picture books are not unknown to me, and I believe I could effect a transmutation.

Perkins … Magic.

Harold Don't be silly, woman.

Mary Ho! Woman, is it?

Harold Mary!

Mary Let's go.

Perkins What? And leave your husband stood here, racked with misery and guilt?

Mary Yes.

Perkins Well I'll be a monkey's …

Mary Come on!

Mary and Perkins exit.

Harold Mary …!
   I taste destruction, I hear
   the thunder of collapsing dreams.
   The world has got the better of me, bloody place.
   And my heart is ripped wide open.
   There is danger here – I sense

disaster – the power of the power
isn't known. A vision! My eyes and ears
give warning of a great catastrophe
if the wrong hands apply this science!
A dream! A nightmare! Cities in ruins!
The oceans run amok! And all our dear ones
hurt, burnt, mutilated.
And at the far end of the garden
now I seem to see
four black-cowled horsemen riding by –
No! Wake me up! Wake me up!

We hear the terrible clatter of hooves and whinnying of horses as the Four Horsemen of the Apocalypse seem to gallop past Harold, over a darkening stage ...

SCENE NINE

Mary and Perkins are in the lab. A swampy sort of bubbling noise. Perkins pokes about.

Perkins What's that? A lizard? What's he want with that?

Mary Entrails, I expect.

Perkins Sort of a goulash, is it?

Mary He predicts the future.

Perkins And so will I! I can barely credit it: absolute knowledge! undreamed of wealth! – This is if you know what you're doing, Mrs.

Mary We need a bucket of water.

Perkins Yeah you would. Four elements. Aristotle.

Mary *(relieved)* Yes. Would you mind, John? The water?

Perkins Knew I'd get lumbered with the legwork.

He brings a bucket of water to Mary.

Mary I like that! I'm the one who's making the big break-out, aren't I? I'm the one who's had the blinding flash, and realised she's been trodden down for all these years.

Perkins You're right. Your mind has come to vibrant life at last, with just a little nudge from me. 'S a giant step, Mrs Lamb, cutting yourself free from the clutching tentacles of the past. Yes. I admire your pluck.

Mary Watch. I'll put some of this sticky red stuff in the bucket.

She pours in some of the elixir of life. She tastes it with her finger.

There. What's happening? I've left my reading specs upstairs.

Perkins It ain't done nothing yet.

Mary Look closer. No, closer.

Perkins *kneels down to peer into the bucket.*

Perkins Well, I think the water's turning red.

Mary Good – that's what it's meant to do. Next, er …

She consults the Wordless Book. Suddenly it speaks to her.

The Wordless Book Begin at the beginning, and end at the end.

Perkins Who said that?

Mary Begin at the beginning, and end at the end?

Perkins Give me the heebie-jeebies.

The Wordless Book Courage, Mrs Lamb!

Mary *(points into the bucket)* There, look!

Perkins What?

Mary Eternity!

Perkins Where?

Mary whacks him over the head with the Wordless Book. His head goes into the liquid. She throws her full weight on top of him to keep him under. Perkins struggles furiously, but Mary is too heavy for him.

Mary Thought you could diddle us, did you, lad?
I know your sort! You're the sort that flushes
the toilet when the train is standing at the station!
You're the sort that gets in the fast queue
with more than nine items in your basket!
You can hear me, can't you?
Just for once it's you that has been had. You see

Perkins' struggles start to subside.

I've weighed up good and bad,
and found, for all his dreaming,
my old Harold's worth twenty of you.

Perkins goes limp. He is dead. Blackout.

SCENE TEN

*The Kitchen. **Mary**, now looking fifty years younger (she's taken off her wig), hums breezily to herself as she makes the tea. **Harold** drifts in from the garden.*

Mary Ah, there you are, Harold.

Harold also looks like a young man. They stare curiously at each other for a brief moment, but do not remark on it.

Want some tea?

Harold Tea?

Mary We're going to be a little late with lunch.

Harold Lunch?

Mary Yes.

Harold But …

Mary The stranger is no longer with us.

Harold But what have you done with him, Mary, love?

Mary I've killed the bugger dead. *(A beat)* A good strong brew is what we need. I know a thing or two about the mysteries of putrefactive fermentation. Hurry up and sit down, dear, we haven't got all day.

Harold Haven't we?

Mary No, we've got to dispose of the body. – Harold didn't you hear? I did a murder. I did a thing entirely on my own. Well aren't you proud of me?

Harold Where is he?

Mary In the cellar with his air-bags full of water. And that gorgeous red potion of yours, that tastes like liquid gold. What is it?

Harold *(admiring Mary's 'new' hair)* Oh, nothing.

Mary We have to go away, my dear. And never tell a soul.

Harold But Mary, wasn't Perkins right? Isn't it immoral? To hide perfection from the world?

Mary You have to ask: what kind of world?

Harold I don't know, I've spent too many years in the lab, perhaps I could improve it, I don't know.

Mary *(laughs)* Improve it? What, those gangsters on the news? The presidents, the generals – you think they can be *improved*? Fat chance. Fat chance, Harold! What's more you can't dis-invent a thing, can you? Once it's there it's there. Even if it's awful!

Harold I've never heard you talk like this before.

Mary Never been scared like this before. Scared enought to actually *do* something ... Harold? What are you weeping for?

Harold *(snuffling)* To come so far ... To find the elixir ...

Mary But what use will the elixir be, living in the ashes of a deep-fried planet? I'd rather perish with the rest!

Harold I didn't know things were so bad.

Mary Well open your eyes, my old, daft lover, open your eyes! They're going berserk out there! They're going ruddy barmy! It's insane! ... Well that's what I think. I know I'm just a housewife. But that's what I think.

Harold I reckon it works. The elixir. I think my eyes are opening ... You'll have to help me, though.

Mary I will. I'm strong.

Harold Oh, Mary ... But what about my garden?

Mary It's too late now for that. It's time to change. If you're to come and live with me, you'll have to learn to cook.

Harold Cook?

Mary Cook. Now drink your tea. The acid bath awaits.

The two of them sip their tea. Fade out.

SCENE ELEVEN

*Perkins' body lies on the floor of the lab. **Mary** stands over it. **Harold** finishes pouring acid into a tin bath. It hisses and steams.*

Mary I'm glad to see you doing something useful for a change. Is it deep enough yet?

Harold Yes.

Mary Right. Do you know, I feel a terrific lot better than I have done for ages. I feel almost young again.

Harold I do too.

Mary I worry a bit, in my bleaker moments, that killing will make me the bigger evil … But then, isn't it nice to get a happy ending, nowadays?

Harold Very nice.

They kiss over the body.

Mary There should be more come-uppance in the world.

Harold Ready?

They drag the body to the acid bath, get its legs over the side, and take an arm each.

One, two, three!

– and they heave the body into the acid. A horrible gurgling sound, and blackout.

The End

ACTIVITIES

FIRST RESPONSES

TALKING POINTS

1 What sort of play is ***Pure Science***?

Work in pairs. One of you will re-tell the story as if it is a fairy tale. Perhaps you could start with something like:

'Once upon a time there was an old man who lived with his old wife. They loved each other very much but the trouble was they just couldn't stop getting older ...'

When this tale comes to an end, the second partner will re-tell it again as if it is a horror story:

'It was just before dawn. Down in the damp, dark cellar an old man was muttering the words of an ancient, magical book ...'

You might find it useful to have a copy of the play open in front of you to remind you of the sequence of events in the story. Don't make your stories too long.

- Talk about which bits of the play might be considered a 'fairy story'. Which bits seem more like a horror story?
- Could the story be re-told in another way?

2 In small groups, talk for a few minutes about anything that surprised you when you read ***Pure Science***.

Divide a large sheet of paper into three columns. Head them:

        CHARACTERS   ACTIONS   LANGUAGE

In each column, jot down your ideas about what makes this play different from any others you know. For example:

Characters	Actions	Language
The Wordless Book	Pouring creosote on rockeries!	Speaking in rhyme

3 Look back at what Nick Dear says about the ideas that lie behind the play for him (page vi).

Which of his words or phrases help explain the play to you? Jot them down. For example:

> I was much concerned with the nuclear threat.

> You can't dis-invent something.

> Science may be pure, or applied.

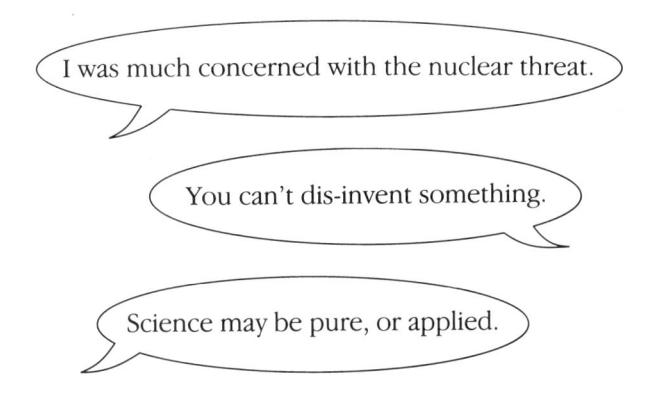

- Do you think science can ever be 'pure' or does it always get turned into something dangerous?
- Re-read Scene Eight. What different opinions do the three characters seem to have about science?

4 *The power of the power
isn't known ...
I seem to see
four black-cowled horsemen riding by –
No! Wake me up! Wake me up!*
                                      page 23

In the last book of the Bible, St John describes the vision he has of the end of the world. At one point he sees four terrifying horses ridden by equally terrifying riders – *'And power was given unto them over the fourth part of the earth, to kill with sword, and with hunger, and with death and with the beasts of the earth'*. Sometimes, these 'four horsemen of the Apocalypse' have been used as a symbol of war and destruction.

- Do you think the play succeeds in warning us about what might happen if scientific discoveries aren't controlled?
- Look at the woodcut overleaf of the four horsemen. How has the artist, Albrecht Dürer, tried to capture the idea of mass destruction?

5 Perkins says *'With all that gold, everyone in the world could give up work!'*

Could they? As a class, discuss:
- Why Perkins might be wrong about this.
- What would happen if everyone suddenly had as much gold as they wanted.

The Four Horsemen of the Apocalypse – a woodcut by Albrecht Dürer 1498

EXPLORING THE LANGUAGE

6 *Did you know there are three hundred and forty thousand different word types in the English language?*

page 5

The storyline of **Pure Science** is concerned with a modern day Alchemist, but the way Nick Dear has written it suggests that language itself can be as magical, powerful and baffling as any chemical concoction.

- Sometimes Nick Dear uses strange words for things. What does he mean, for example, by *pedal extremity* (p. 9), or *have a butchers* (p. 17)? Flick through the play and try to pick out some other expressions or words in the play which are quirky. Jot them down then, in brackets underneath, write what you think they mean in your own words.
- Talk about why the characters in this play might use such strange language. Is it that complicated ideas need complicated language? Perhaps some words and phrases are simply just more fun to say than others. You may have come across people who use difficult language simply to make others feel stupid and powerless. Are the characters in **Pure Science** like this?
- As a class, make a chart like the one below which reflects some of your reactions to the way language is used in your own lives:

Ideas that are difficult to put into words	Our favourite sayings and words	Types of people who use language to put us down.

7 Re-read Harold's speech on page 4 then look at the chart overleaf which compares Nick Dear's writing to one possible explanation of what it means.

- Write an explanation of the rest of Harold's speech using a chart like this.
- Compare the 'logical' version with the original by reading them both aloud.
- Which one (a) sounds more interesting?
  (b) is easier to understand?
  (c) tells us more about Harold?
- Do you think you should be able to understand the language

33

of plays immediately or is there enjoyment to be had just listening to the way words are played with? (You should of course remember that plays are written to be performed rather than only read.)

HAROLD'S SPEECH	EXPLANATION
For you suffer me with a laughing heart	Your love makes you patient with me
and guide me through the darkest tunnels of the night.	even when I get very very depressed.
One day this great work will be finished, and then we shall fear no more the cold and the damp of the box in the earth or the heat of the white hot furnace.	One day I'll find what I'm looking for and then we won't worry about dying and being either buried or cremated.
The world, beyond the trellis at the bottom of the lawn, is a sour place, full of bitter people.	?

8 Find another speech from the play that you think uses language in an interesting and imaginative way.

Either try to describe why the language is effective. Think about:
- what the words remind you of.
- what sort of rhythm the speech has.
- what you learn about the character through the way the speech is written.

Or, tape record yourself reading the speech in different ways. Try reading it:
- slowly/quickly
- softly/loudly
- talking as if you are just having a conversation/really emphasising the rhythm by paying attention to the length of each line.

WRITE

9 Nick Dear writes:

As far as I can tell all formulae are gibberish whether they're for sodium tetrachloride or the Elixir of life.
- Read the passage from 'The Wordless Book' on page 2. What effect does it have on you as a reader?
- Write another page from 'The Wordless Book' in a style which seems to say 'this really makes sense but you're just too thick to understand it'!

10 *Palindrome. Reads the same word-wise forwards or backwards. Try it.*

page 5
- Work as a whole class to collect as many individual words as possible together which can be read backwards.
- Now try making very short sentences which mean the same when read backwards as forwards. Eve might have heard another example in the Garden of Eden when a man came up and said 'Madam, I'm Adam'.!
- Perkins' second 'game' was to try to make a sentence using all 26 letters of the alphabet. See if you can make one.
- Another 'word game' you might try is telling a story in which the first letter of each word follows on in alphabetical order. For example:

> **Andy's brother could dance each Friday ...**

DRAMA

11 In pairs, improvise one of the following scenes using the story of **Pure Science** as a basis:
- A is a neighbour of Harold and Mary who has complained to the police about the 'strange goings-on' in their house. B is a police officer who has come to take the details.
- A is a TV newsreader in the studio talking to B who is an 'on-the spot reporter' outside the house where, it is reported, some unusual things have been happening.
- A is Mrs Perkins who is looking for her husband who seems to have disappeared. B is a now young Mary (or Harold) who decides to tell Mrs Perkins the truth about what happened.
- Invent two other characters who would, for some reason, 're-tell' the events of this play. Share your work with the rest of the class.

12 At the end of ***Pure Science*** Harold and Mary miraculously start becoming younger again. In Shakespeare's play *As You Like It* one of the characters says that there are seven ages in a person's life. Working in small groups:
- Invent a character and pick seven 'key' events in his or her life.
- Act them out at double speed as if their life was being played on 'fast forward'.
- Now 'rewind' their life as if they had taken some of Harold's special potion.

Each scene must be very simple and clear. Try to pick out a key action and just two or three key lines for each event (but don't bother trying to say the lines backwards for goodness sake!)

13 Look back to the picture of The Four Horsemen of the Apocalypse. The nightmarish vision seems to show a great destructive power being unleashed.
- In groups of four, jot down two or three words or phrases which come to mind when you look at the picture.
- Decide an order for your words and phrases.
- Go through them slowly and softly, then again slightly louder and faster. Build up the pace and the volume.
- Think about how you might add movement and other sounds in order to make a 'dramatic' representation of this picture.

EXPLORING THE CHARACTERS

PERKINS

1 Nick Dear describes Perkins as:
a hard nut in a polyester suit. I wouldn't be surprised if his fingernails were disgusting.

Mary says:
I know your sort! You're the sort that flushes the toilet when the train is standing at the station!

Draw a sketch of Perkins and label the bits of his body and clothing that you would find offputting. Underneath, you might note some other repulsive habits and characteristics he has!

2 Look back at scenes 6, 7 and 8.
- Jot down a number of words or phrases of your own that seem to sum up Perkins's character for you.
- If you were to research into Perkins's past life, who would

you want to talk to? As a whole class, decide on six key people in his life. Agree on some basic details about, for example, their name and age. Don't get bogged down inventing their characters – it's Perkins that we are interested in.

- Six class members should sit at points around the room. The rest of the class 'hot-seat' them to find out what they know and think about Perkins.
- Did all of the characters say the same sort of thing about Perkins? Was their view of him the same as yours? How could you explain these differences of opinion?

3 Read pages 5–7 again. Perkins has a number of 'techniques' which he uses to try and trick his way into Mary's house. Imagine that Perkins is known to the police as a small-time con-man. Working in small groups, make up a 'dossier' on him. The file will include statements taken from past victims describing how he tricked them. Here is a copy of a police statement form which you could use as a 'frame' for your work.

HAPPY VALLEY POLICE

Witness Statement

Statement of ....

Age if under 21 .... (if over 21 insert 'over 21').

This statement (consisting of   pages each signed by me) is true to the best of my knowledge and belief and I make it knowing that, if it is tendered in evidence, I shall be liable to prosecution if I have wilfully stated in it anything which I know to be false or do not believe to be true.

Dated the   day of   19

Signature ....

....

....

....

Signature .... Signature witnessed by ....

- Display the statements about Perkins and discuss the different approaches other writers in the class have taken.

Have some tried to gain our sympathy for the victims? Are others funny or do they perhaps celebrate Perkins's devious character?

- What other documents might be in Perkins's police file? A 'watch out for this man' poster? His school report? A reference from a probation officer?

4 How would Perkins deal with different types of 'customers'? His aim, remember, is to try and sell a set of encyclopaedias and get whatever else out of his victims he can.

- In pairs, one of you is Perkins and the other plays one of the following 'customers':
  - A very suspicious Crimewatch fan.
  - Someone who looks uncomfortably like Freddy Kruger (or any other sinister character from a horror film).
  - The winner of last year's Mastermind competition.
  - A very rude child.
  - Someone with several screaming children hanging around their legs.

  After improvising a scene for a few minutes, stop and start a new scene with a new partner playing a different character. (You may, of course, choose to invent your own 'difficult customers'.)

- Imagine that Perkins sets up an evening class for door-to-door salesmen in order to help them get the best results. Work as a whole class. Pairs take it in turns to share examples of scenes created above. In role as members of the evening class, the rest of the group offer advice on how to polish up their technique.

5 Perkins seems like a stereotypical crooked door-to-door salesman. It's easy to laugh at such a character but does he actually have a more serious function in the play? Look at his speeches on pages 11 and 17.

- Do you think that he's right when he says *'There's always someone wants to suss the secrets of the universe'*?
- What books or products do you know of that offer people a short cut to 'self-advancement' and 'life-enhancement'?
- Talk about the type of knowledge that Perkins actually has (*'Did you know a dying octopus often eats its own arms?'*). How useful is this sort of knowledge? Why do you think people seem to be so fascinated by 'trivia'?

HAROLD AND MARY

6 In groups, copy the outline of Harold and Mary onto a large sheet of paper. Inside the outline, jot down what you actually know about them. Around the outside of the outline jot down any assumptions you would make about them.

Harold and Mary

7 Nick Dear writes about Harold and Mary that:

'Their general manner is that of everybody's favourite grandparents.'

It would be easy to stereotype Harold and Mary as doddery old codgers who walked with a stoop and talked in a shaky old voice about 'the good old days' *but*
- Do your grandparents or other old people you know fit such a stereotype?
- Draw a simple outline of either Harold or Mary onto a piece of card and cut it out (you could adapt the drawing above). On one side, jot down ways in which the character is a 'typical' old codger. On the other side note down ways in which they seem more like individuals. You might choose to jot down some lines from the play.
- Display the cards like a mobile – it will make a change from putting things on the wall and in a way it will show more effectively that characters are made up from a number of different viewpoints!

8 Using the ideas generated above, imagine what photos Harold and Mary might have on their mantelpiece or in a photograph album. Work in groups using yourselves to present a pictorial history of their life together. Imagine that Harold and Mary are looking at the photographs – what would they say about each one? Perhaps some photographs bring out the 'old codger' in them whereas others trigger individual memories and thoughts.

9 In groups, prepare and show one of the following improvisations. Try to keep the characterisations of Harold and Mary consistent with the way they are presented in ***Pure Science***.
- When Harold first takes the elixir we are told that: *'Several of his teeth have fallen out, as have great tufts of his hair. He is blackened with smoke.'* Imagine that rather than dealing with Perkins, Mary drags Harold off to the doctor's surgery. Improvise the scene there.
- Having taken the elixir Harold and Mary have started to become younger instead of older. What happens when they meet a neighbour who has noticed the change and says: 'My! You're looking well! Whatever have you been taking'?

- Imagine that Perkins's body is found and Harold and Mary admit murdering him. Improvise a scene in which the lawyer is interviewing Harold and Mary. The first line might be: 'Now then Mr and Mrs Lamb. You've admitted that you murdered Mr Perkins. Your only hope in court is to explain exactly why you did it. So, can you tell me?'

10 If Harold and Mary were to *'go away. And never tell a soul'*, how do you think the story of their disappearance would be told in the local paper?

PERFORMING THE PLAY

FROM RADIO TO STAGE

> *Pure Science* was originally produced as a radio play. On the radio, characters such as The Wordless Book, Harold's Belly and An Ancient Chinese Philosopher wouldn't pose much of a problem; the audience just needs to hear their lines.
>
> On stage though, these characters might present both challenges and opportunities. The challenge is how to introduce them without breaking the flow of the play? The opportunity is there though to use the characters to surprise and delight an audience.

1 Discuss or experiment with these options for presenting The Wordless Book, then consider how you would present the other 'odd' characters.
   - An actor offstage using a microphone to speak the lines that Harold is 'reading' in his 'dusty ledger'. What sort of voice should be used? Are there any tricks you can play with the sound system to make the voice more interesting?
   - An actor comes on stage to speak the lines (or perhaps stays on stage the whole time). What should the actor wear? How should he stand and what should he do?
   - Harold simply reads the lines himself from the book.
   - The 'dusty ledger' that the actor playing Harold picks up has got coloured foil stuck to its pages. When he opens the book, the stage lights dim but one small spot light positioned above and slightly behind him reflects the colour of the foil onto his face. 'Magically', as he turns the pages, the colour of his face changes. Either he or an offstage actor speaks the words.

large 'antique' book

coloured foil

minispot focused on book

> When **Pure Science** was first performed on stage a problem had to be solved about how to show Harold and Mary growing younger; this obviously wasn't such a problem on the radio where the words alone could be made to conjure up a picture in the listeners' heads. Nick Dear's solution was to suggest that Harold and Mary are played by young actors in grey wigs and make-up.

2 If you were to produce **Pure Science**, how convincing do you think Harold and Mary's make-up would need to be? Would it, in fact, be possible to make up such young actors convincingly? Would it matter if the audience could see that the actors were young people made up to look old?

If possible, make up two volunteers as Harold and two as Mary. One couple should be made up as realistically as possible; the other should be made up in a way that simply 'suggests' that they are old.

Compare the results and discuss which method you think would work best in a production.

> **Pure Science** needs to be acted in three areas: the kitchen, the garden and the laboratory. Switching from one scene to another isn't a big problem in a radio play. On stage, all three areas should be seen at once so that the action can switch from one to the other with the minimum of pause. In some plays this would ruin the atmosphere but Nick Dear says that **Pure Science** isn't 'a naturalistic play'.

DESIGNING THE SET

3 Discuss the different ways of dividing an acting area into three. Would you, for example, simply divide the stage into three equal areas? Or could you use different levels to suggest the three locations?
- Sketch a number of solutions which show how your performance space could be split into three. Think about height and depth as well as the floor space.
- Make a list of where each scene takes place. Now write which characters appear in each scene. Look at your sketches and check to see if it will be possible for the actors to move from one scene to the next easily. For example, would Harold be able to get from the garden (Scene One) to the laboratory (Scene Three) without walking through the kitchen where Mary is in Scene two?
- Decide which sketch would probably work best in the space you have. Draw in some simple signs to show what objects you would put in the kitchen and garden. Add a brief description of the objects.

plain wooden table with yellow formica top

Kitchen chairs: wooden with red plastic seats

4 Nick Dear says that *'a great deal of naturalistic detail is not necessary'* but he describes the laboratory as *'a hissing, wheezing wonderland of ovens, flasks and phials, ancient books and peculiar smells'*.
- Look at the picture on page v at the front of the book. What sort of sounds and movements are suggested? In small groups, present an image of an alchemical laboratory using your bodies and sounds (but not words) to capture the atmosphere.

43

- Keep this atmosphere in mind and write your own detailed description of Harold's laboratory using what you know from the play but adding everything else that you think might possibly be in there.
- Now sketch or describe how you could 'suggest' Harold's laboratory in a simple but effective way for a production of **Pure Science**.

5 Look back to Scene Five in which Harold finally discovers 'the Elixir of life'.

The stage direction says that *'the equipment's going berserk'*. What ideas have you got for:
- making jars and pans rattle on stage?
- giving the impression that various liquids were bubbling?
- making liquids in glass jars change colour?
- creating sparks and smoke?

Above all else, how would you make sure that these effects were safe?

ALCHEMY

ALCHEMISTS AND PUFFERS

Interior of a Puffer's Laboratory by Peter Breughel the Elder

According to old books on the subject, the alchemist had to go on a very special kind of journey which involved 'praying theosophically and working physico-chemically'. The successful alchemist ends his journey in a 'citadel' which has seven corners which he must visit:

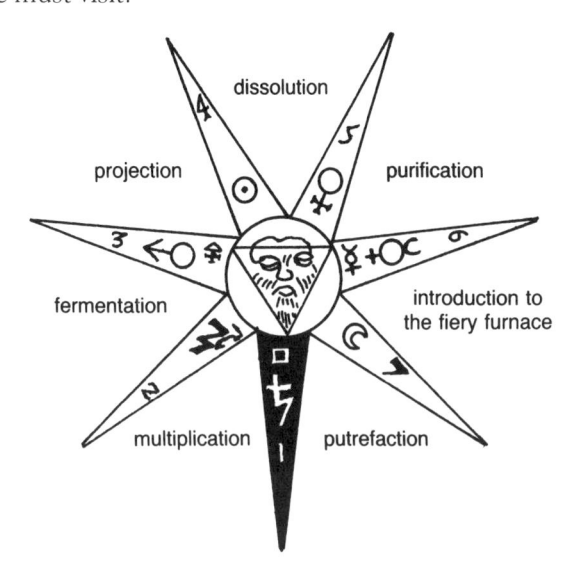

Diagram of a seven-pointed star with labels: dissolution, purification, introduction to the fiery furnace, putrefaction, multiplication, fermentation, projection.

Finally, the famous Philosopher's Stone is reached, but it is guarded by a dragon which only gives the secret to those who have accomplished all the required operations. 'False' alchemists or 'Puffers' spent their lives experimenting only with solid substances and ignoring what the processes of 'true' alchemy might mean to the way they thought *and* felt. 'True' alchemists sought to understand Nature by imitating it rather than trying to cheat it. One fifteenth century alchemist who claimed to have found the Philosphers' Stone wrote:

> *Thou wilt do as I did it if thou wilt take pains to be what thou shouldest be – that is to say, pious, gentle, benign, charitable, and fearing God.*

1 Look at the picture which shows a 'Puffer's' laboratory.
  ♦ In groups of five or six, adopt the poses of the characters in the scene and bring it to life for a few minutes. What are they saying to each other?
  ♦ Imagine that the man seated at the desk is the 'Puffer', that is, someone who is trying to use experiments just to make new

substances rather than rise into a higher spiritual plane. His experiments have been going very badly and he is on the point of giving up. If he left the laboratory, how would the conversation amongst the others change? Act out the scene.

- The person who is playing the Alchemist can choose when he or she wants to re-enter. How does this reappearance affect the conversation?

2 Read the extract below. It is a translation from *The Canon's Yeoman's Tale*, which was written over 600 years ago. In it the poet Chaucer describes an incredible list of 'ingredients' used in an attempt to find the Stone.

Now, a proper education I certainly missed
So I can't give you an ordered list
Of all the different things our curious trade
Demanded that we bought, or found or made.
So, notwithstanding their various class or kind
This is how they come into my mind:
Clay from Armenia, borax and verdigris,
Glass pots, earthenware pots and pots full of pee,
Pots of all sizes for extracting oil,
A crucible to test that the mix doesn't spoil
Beakers, phials, a distiller's retort,
Tons of other paraphenalia all of that sort;
All absolutely worthless, I couldn't name it all.
Rubified water, a stone from a bullock's gall,
Amonia and brimstone, not to mention arsenic,
The herbs we'd use would fill many a sack;
Agrimony, moonwort, valerian and stuff,
I could tell you more if you cared enough.
We had the lamps burning night and day
To help us find that elusive way.
For calcification, the furnace burned bright,
While albefaction turned water quite white
(With the help of chalk and lime, ashes and eggs.
Nameless powders, clay, piss, dung and dregs).
There were bagfulls of wax, saltpetre and vitriol,
Fires made from all sorts of wood or coal
Alkali, tartar, salts in different mode
Stuff stuck together or about to explode.
Mud mixed with horse-hair, and sometimes my own,
Alum turned to crystal or tartar that's thrown
Together with sour and unfermented beer
And things about which you won't want to hear . . .

Imagine that you work for someone who is determined to find the Philosopher's Stone. Occasionally he gives you a shopping list of things to get for his next attempt at the Great Work. Write what's on the list.

3 Work in pairs and improvise one of the following scenes:
- A is the assistant who has the list written above.
  B is a local shopkeeper specialising in supplying alchemists.
- A is a travelling salesperson for a company of alchemical equipment manufacturers.
  B is an increasingly disappointed and frustrated alchemist who has had a series of disasters in his work.

Share some examples of these scenes and discuss how people have used language to show their characters and situation.

4 One of the reasons why the Canon's Yeoman says that alchemy is so expensive is because a great many people were tricked by men who claimed to be able to turn base metals into gold for a fee. In 1612, the great English dramatist Ben Jonson wrote a play about how people's greed encouraged such con-men. Here is how he introduces the play. Notice how he is also playing tricks with the language:

> **T**he sickness hot, a master quit, for fear,
> **H**is house in town, and left one servant there.
> **E**ase him corrupted, and gave means to know
> **A** Cheater and his punk, who now brought low
> **L**eaving their narrow practice, were become
> **C**oz'ners at large; and only wanting some
> **H**ouse to set up, with him they here contract,
> **E**ach for a share, and all begin to act.
> **M**uch company they draw, and much abuse,
> **I**n casting figures, telling fortunes, news,
> **S**elling of flies, flat bawdry, with the Stone;

- This introduction tells you the basic plot of the play. Read it through again and discuss what you think the story is all about.

- Write your own poem or story about either someone who is tricked because they are so greedy, or someone who makes a living out of tricking greedy people. You could try writing an *acrostic* – that is, a poem in which the first letters of each line spell something out.

THE APPLIANCE OF SCIENCE

5 Would you want to live forever? Imagine that you are offered the opportunity of drinking the 'elixir of life'. What thoughts might hold you back?

You may know the story of Jekyll and Hyde. In it, a doctor discovers a drug which can separate the good and bad parts of his personality. Unfortunately, rather than being destroyed, the bad part gradually takes him over with horrific consequences …

Imagine that the mixture Harold has manufactured has some unexpected side effects. Improvise or script a new last scene for **Pure Science**.

6 When it was pointed out to Albert Einstein that his theories had led to the development of the atomic bomb, he is reported to have said 'If I'd known I would have been a locksmith'.
- Research into other real scientific experiments that have gone terribly wrong or had unforeseen consequences.
- Talk, or write about, what responsibilities you think scientists should have.
- Devise a short play or story about a scientist who discovers something he wishes he hadn't but then can't 'dis-invent' it.

7 Look at the 'blurb' on the back cover of this book. You will see that it is presented in three parts.
- Jot down what the *function* of each section is.
- Imagine that there is another play in this series which explores the result of a scientific experiment. Perhaps it is about an amazing new invention or some discovery that will change the way people think. Write a blurb for this new play using this same format.

DR FAUSTUS

A GRISLY TALE

There are many stories of people who have gone to extremes in the quest for knowledge and eternal life. Some are said to have made pacts with the Devil. One such story is about a certain Dr Faustus who is believed to have lived in Germany in the early sixteenth century. The first version of his story was published in 1548. The legend grew until eventually an English version was published in 1592 under the title *The Historie of the damnable life, and deserved death of Doctor John Faustus*. In the story, Faustus promises his soul to the Devil in return for 24 years of life during which a demon called Mephistopheles shall give him whatever he wants. When the 24 years are up, Faustus waits, terrified of whatever the Devil has in store for him. According to the book, some students who knew of his pact were staying nearby:

> ... they heard a mighty noise and hissing, as if the hall had been full of snakes and adders. With that the hall door flew open wherein Doctor Faustus was; then he began to cry for help saying, 'Murder, murder'! But it came forth with half a voice hollowly; shortly after, they heard him no more. But when it was day, the students, that had taken no rest that night, arose and went into the hall in the which they left Doctor Faustus; where notwithstanding they found no Faustus; but all the hall lay besprinkled with blood, his brains cleaving to the wall; for the devil had beaten him from one wall against another; in one corner lay his eyes, in another his teeth, a pitiful and fearful sight to behold. Then began the students to bewail and weep for him and sought for his body in many places. Lastly they came into the yard where they found his body lying on the horse dung, most montrously torn and fearful to behold; for his head and all his joints were dashed in pieces.

1 ***Pure Science*** could be described as a 'black comedy'. We don't feel sorry for Perkins when he's murdered, in fact, the way Mary does it, it seems quite funny.

The story of Faustus certainly wasn't originally written to make people laugh. It was written as a warning about what happens to people like Faustus who are driven by greed and ambition to be more than God meant them to be. In the sixteenth century, the students' story of how Faustus met his grisly end would probably have been believed, but what would people's reaction be today?

In small groups, improvise the following scenes:
- Imagine that you are the students mentioned in this extract. Improvise the scene and the conversation in their room on the night of Faustus's death. Make it clear why they didn't go to help him.
- Improvise the scene in which they sought for his body in many places ...
- Act out a scene in a modern police station in which the students report the death of their friend Dr Faustus.

2 The first play about Dr Faustus was by Christopher Marlowe sometime around 1592. (Marlowe himself met a pretty horrible end in a knife-fight. Some said that he was mixed up with various spying activities and others that he denied the existence of God.) Read this extract from the end of the play:

The clock strikes eleven.

Ah, Faustus,
Now hast thou but one bare hour to live,
And then thou must be damn'd perpetually.
Stand still, you ever-moving spheres of heaven,
That time may cease, and midnight never come;
Fair nature's eye, rise, rise again, and make
A year, a month, a week, a natural day,
That Faustus may repent and save his soul.
O lente lente currite noctis equi!
(Run slowly slowly O horses of the night)
The stars move still, time runs, the clock will strike,
The devil will come, and Faustus must be damn'd.

In pairs, talk about what you think Faustus is saying here. Read it through again, taking it in turns to read the lines. Try reading it:
- quietly, as if you are talking to yourself.
- sadly, as if you have already given up any hope.
- angrily, knowing that you have put yourself in this position.
- pleadingly, hoping that someone will hear and save you.
- melodramatically, as if you are really just trying to impress the audience.
- Try out some other ways of your own to read it. Which do you think is the most effective?

Gösta Ekman

- Having decided on the best sort of voice, work together on Faustus's movements, gestures and expressions. What would you want an audience to actually see while the actor is speaking these lines?

3 Look at the pictures on page 51. They show the different ways Faustus has been imagined.
   - Do all of these pictures seem to show the same kind of person? Talk about the different characters that seem to be shown here.
   - Imagine Faustus as the man that has just sold himself to the devil in order to be able to do, know and see things that other people couldn't. He has 24 years stretching out in front of him. If you were to play Faustus on stage, how would you play him? Make a few notes using the chart below as a guide:
   - Sketch some designs for Faustus's costume and study which would fit in with your vision of him.
   - Compare your idea of Faustus with Harold in **Pure Science**. Jot down what you think the similarities are. If you can only see differences, jot down why they are different.
   - Talk about your notes with a partner.

Attitude towards others …
Attitude towards himself …
What does he want most of all?
What does he fear most of all?
How does he like to dress?
What are the favourite things in his study?

COMEDY OR TRAGEDY?

4 Marlowe called his play *The Tragical History of the Life and Death of Doctor Faustus*. In fact, there are many parts of the play which can be very funny on stage – after all, Faustus can do *anything* he wants including flying, being invisible and summoning up people from other times and places.
   - In groups, devise a comic scene of your own in which a character has limitless power.
   - Share your scenes and discuss how the comedy works. Is it the situation that is funny, or what happens to certain people in it?

5   At the end of Marlowe's play Dr Faustus gets his comeuppance for dabbling with the Devil. Do you think Harold should get his comeuppance at the end of *Pure Science*?

Devise a new scene which shows either how Harold is punished for his scientific dabbling or why he isn't.

6   It has been said that *'the world is a tragedy to those who feel, a comedy to those who think'*.

Do you think it would be good to *only* think about the world and never experience feelings? Are there dangers in being forever at the mercy of your feelings and never actually thinking?

- Without discussion, work as a group to brainstorm two lists under the headings comic and tragic. Keep writing for at least three minutes.

- Look at the two lists and discuss what you have written in terms of *characters* or *situations*. For example, is it always funny when somebody slips on a banana skin, or does the comedy depend on who they are?

- What would need to change in *Pure Science* to make it a tragedy? Re-write or improvise a scene from the play which changes the tone of it to one that is essentially tragic.

Titles in the Dramascripts Extra Series

In Search of Dragon's Mountain
Toeckey Jones
0-17-432350-6

Moll Flanders
Claire Luckham
Adapted by Lib Taylor
0-17-432349-2

Sherlock Holmes and the Limehouse Horror
Philip Pullman
0-17-432347-6

No Man's Land
Paul Swift
0-17-432348-4

A Feeling in my Bones
Lin Coghlan
0-17-432346-8

Anansi
Alistair Campbell
0-17-432345-X

Gulliver
Brian Woolland
0-17-432486-3

Pure Science
Nick Dear
0-17-432487-1

The Travels of Yoshi and the Tea Kettle
Lynne Reid Banks
0-17-432488-X

The Last Laugh
Ben Payne
0-17-432489-8